dinosaur
detectives'
handbook

dinosaur detectives' handbook

Miles Kelly

PUBLISHING

First published in 2006 by
Miles Kelly Publishing Ltd
Bardfield Centre, Great Bardfield, Essex, CM7 4SL

Copyright © Miles Kelly Publishing Ltd 2006

This edition printed in 2007

2 4 6 8 10 9 7 5 3

Editorial Director Belinda Gallagher

Art Director Jo Brewer

Editorial Assistant Bethanie Bourne

Design Concept Candice Bekir

Designers Candice Bekir, Samantha South

Picture Research Manager Liberty Newton

Picture Researcher Laura Faulder

Production Elizabeth Brunwin

Reprographics Anthony Cambray, Mike Coupe, Stephan Davis, Ian Paulyn

ISBN 13: 978-1-84236-729-2

Printed in China

British Library Cataloguing-in-Publication Data
A catalogue record for this book is available
from the British Library

www.mileskelly.net
info@mileskelly.net

All artworks are from MKP Archives

CONTENTS

How to use your book   6
What is a dinosaur?   8
Digging up dinosaurs   10

Allosaurus   12
Ankylosaurus   14
Apatosaurus   16
Avimimus   18
Barosaurus   20
Baryonyx   22
Brachiosaurus   24
Camarasaurus   26
Caudipteryx   28
Ceratosaurus   30
Coelophysis   32
Compsognathus   34
Corythosaurus   36
Deinonychus   38
Dilophosaurus   40
Edmontonia   42
Eustreptospondylus   44
Giganotosaurus   46
Herrerasaurus   48
Hypsilophodon   50
Iguanodon   52
Janenschia   54
Jobaria   56
Kentrosaurus   58

Lambeosaurus   60
Leaellynasaura   62
Maiasaura   64
Megalosaurus   66
Muttaburrasaurus   68
Ornitholestes   70
Ornithomimus   72
Oviraptor   74
Pachycephalosaurus   76
Parasaurolophus   78
Plateosaurus   80
Polacanthus   82
Procompsognathus   84
Protoceratops   86
Psittacosaurus   88
Riojasaurus   90
Saltasaurus   92
Shunosaurus   94
Spinosaurus   96
Stegosaurus   98
Syntarsus   100
Triceratops   102
Troodon   104
Tuojiangosaurus   106
Tyrannosaurus rex   108
Velociraptor   110

Glossary   112

HOW TO USE YOUR BOOK

Use this guide to help you find your way around the book. There's information about each dinosaur, maps to show where their fossils have been found, and lots of amazing facts. You can add your own notes and pictures to the write-in area.

This provides you with lots of information – from how much dinosaurs weighed to how you should pronounce their names.

PERIOD COLOURS

These tell you exactly what time period each dinosaur lived in.
Orange = Triassic Period
Blue = Jurassic Period
Green = Cretaceous Period

Use these boxes to find out where in the world dinosaur fossil sites have been located.

Find out amazing information about each dinosaur.

This is a write-in area for you to draw pictures and jot down your own notes, ideas and thoughts about each dinosaur.

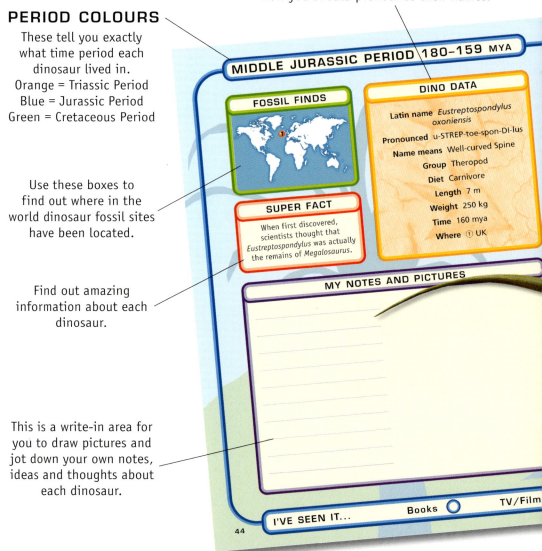

MIDDLE JURASSIC PERIOD 180–159 MYA

FOSSIL FINDS

DINO DATA

Latin name Eustreptospondylus oxoniensis
Pronounced u-STREP-toe-spon-DI-lus
Name means Well-curved Spine
Group Theropod
Diet Carnivore
Length 7 m
Weight 250 kg
Time 160 mya
Where ① UK

SUPER FACT

When first discovered, scientists thought that Eustreptospondylus was actually the remains of Megalosaurus.

MY NOTES AND PICTURES

I'VE SEEN IT...   Books ⬭   TV/Film

44

PULL-OUT POSTER PLUS 50 STICKERS

TIMELINE POSTER

Stick this to a wall or door. Now you can see all the dinosaurs in this book, and the time periods they lived in.

STICKER SHEETS

All the dinosaurs are supplied as stickers. Place them where you like in the book, or make your own sticker album.

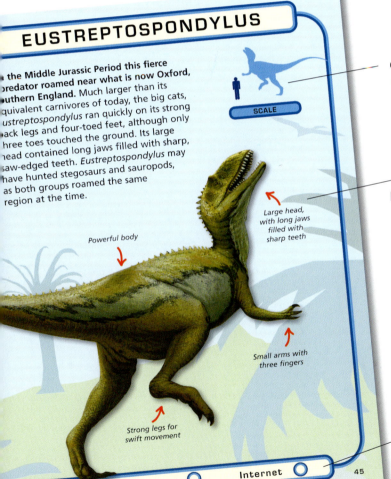

EUSTREPTOSPONDYLUS

In the Middle Jurassic Period this fierce predator roamed near what is now Oxford, southern England. Much larger than its equivalent carnivores of today, the big cats, *Eustreptospondylus* ran quickly on its strong back legs and four-toed feet, although only three toes touched the ground. Its large head contained long jaws filled with sharp, saw-edged teeth. *Eustreptospondylus* may have hunted stegosaurs and sauropods, as both groups roamed the same region at the time.

SCALE

Large head, with long jaws filled with sharp teeth

Powerful body

Small arms with three fingers

Strong legs for swift movement

Museums ○   Internet ○   45

You can see exactly how big, or small, each dinosaur was compared to people, by looking at the scale area.

FACTFILE

Every right-hand page has a dinosaur factfile and picture. Read the main paragraph to find out about each dinosaur. The labels give you extra information.

Keep a record of your dinosaur sightings and tick the circles when you've 'seen' a dinosaur. Keep a note of any other places you've come across one.

WHAT IS A DINOSAUR?

The dinosaurs were a group of prehistoric reptiles that held their legs directly beneath their bodies, like modern mammals. Dinosaurs were closely related to crocodiles. It is thought that birds probably evolved from one type of dinosaur.

HOW TO IDENTIFY A DINOSAUR

1 Legs are held directly under the body, not sprawling sideways as in other reptiles.

2 The ankle has a simple joint that allows limited movements, unlike most other reptiles, which have ankles capable of twisting in all directions.

3 Hips are joined solidly to the backbone, not loosely, as is more usual in reptiles.

4 Long hind legs. Nearly all dinosaurs had hind legs that were significantly longer than their front legs.

Hips joined solidly to backbone

Simple ankle

▶ *Dinosaurs ruled the land for about 150 million years. This is longer than any other animal group. The Age of Dinosaurs is called the Mesozoic Era. This huge time span is broken down into three smaller chunks of time – the Triassic, Jurassic and Cretaceous Periods. The dinosaurs first appeared towards the end of the Triassic Period. During the Jurassic Period, dinosaurs reached their greatest size. The dinosaurs were at their most varied during the Cretaceous Period.*

YEARS AGO (MILLIONS)	ERA	PERIOD
80	MESOZOIC (AGE OF DINOSAURS)	CRETACEOUS
100		CRETACEOUS
120		CRETACEOUS
140		JURASSIC
160		JURASSIC
180		JURASSIC
200		JURASSIC
220		TRIASSIC

LIZARD-HIPPED OR BIRD-HIPPED?

Dinosaurs form a large group of reptiles called the Dinosauria. This group is then divided into two smaller groups known as Saurischia and Ornithischia, mainly on the basis of their hip structure, which is either lizard-hipped or bird-hipped.

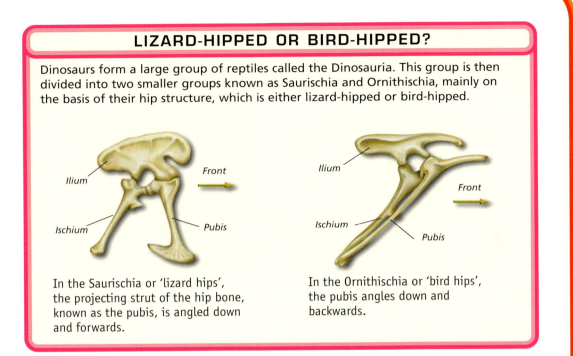

In the Saurischia or 'lizard hips', the projecting strut of the hip bone, known as the pubis, is angled down and forwards.

In the Ornithischia or 'bird hips', the pubis angles down and backwards.

WHAT DOES HIP STRUCTURE TELL US?

Hip structure tells us if a dinosaur was a plant eater or a meat eater. All of the meat-eating dinosaurs, and a few plant eaters, were lizard hips. All bird-hipped dinosaurs were plant eaters.

SAURISCHIA (LIZARD HIPS)

THEROPODS (beast feet) This group includes meat eaters and some plant eaters. However, nearly all were meat eaters that walked on two legs, with three toes on each foot.

SAUROPODS (lizard feet) All were plant eaters, with long necks, bulky bodies, long tails and pillar-like legs.

ORNITHISCHIA (BIRD HIPS)

This group was purely plant eaters.

ORNITHOPODS (bird feet)

STEGOSAURS (roofed or plated reptiles)

ANKYLOSAURS (armoured reptiles)

PACHYCEPHALOSAURS (bone heads)

CERATOPSIANS (horn faces)

DIGGING UP DINOSAURS

We know about dinosaurs because of their fossils. These are their remains that were buried after death in mud, sand or similar materials. They were then preserved in rocks over millions of years, and gradually turned to stone. Not only dinosaurs, but many kinds of plants and animals have left behind fossils.

◄ *A fossilized claw of Baryonyx. Fossils such as this provide palaeontologists (scientists who study fossilized remains) with huge amounts of information about the way a dinosaur lived – and what it may have looked like.*

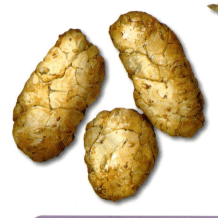

◄ *Usually only the hardest parts of living things form fossils. For dinosaurs these are mainly bones, teeth, horns and claws. The softer parts such as muscles, nerves and even skin were soon eaten by scavengers or rotted away. However, fossilized dinosaur dung has been discovered. These fossils are called coprolites.*

LOOKING AT DINOSAURS

Fossils are not original living material, but rock and stone, made of minerals. So a fossil's colour is that of its minerals. This means we cannot tell the colour of dinosaurs. Some may have been camouflaged brown and green, like alligators and turtles today. Others may have been colourful, like some living lizards and snakes.

Stegosaurus may have had brightly coloured skin

1 *Palaeontologists chip away rock covering the fossil. They may have to cut a deep trench in the surrounding rock to free the fossil.*

2 *Detailed diagrams and maps of the fossil positions are drawn up before any fossils are moved. These act as important documents when fossils are back in the laboratory.*

3 *Some fossils are carefully wrapped to protect them on their journey from the fossil site back to the laboratory.*

4 *At the laboratory, staff clean and study the fossils with care. It is rare to find a skeleton with all the bones arranged as they were in life. Usually the remains are crushed or broken, with parts missing. Great skill is needed to piece the fossils together. Often fossils from similar dinosaurs are used to fill in missing parts.*

5 *Once a dinosaur skeleton is reconstructed as far as possible, experts begin to guess how it looked in life. Marks on bones called muscle scars show where muscles were attached, their size and lines of pull. Studies of dinosaur cousins alive today, such as crocodiles, are used for comparison of soft body parts. Gradually the skeleton is cloaked in flesh.*

▲ *Scientists study rocks to find out their type and age. Dinosaur fossils occur in the rocks of the Mesozoic Era. Palaeontologists survey an area to see if fossils are present. If remains are found, they dig and chip out the fossils with care. Every stage of the excavation or 'dig' is recorded with notes, diagrams and photos.*

FOSSIL FINDS

DINO DATA

Latin name *Allosaurus fragilis*

Pronounced aL-o-SAW-rus

Name means Different Reptile

Group Theropod

Diet Carnivore

Length 12 m

Weight 2 tonnes

Time 150 mya

Where ① USA, ② Africa, ③ Australia

SUPER FACT

The huge teeth of *Allosaurus* curved backwards to prevent its struggling prey from escaping its massive jaws.

MY NOTES AND PICTURES

I'VE SEEN IT...   Books ○   TV/Films ○

ALLOSAURUS

The largest meat eater of the Late Jurassic Period, *Allosaurus* would have rivalled *T Rex* in size. This fierce hunter preyed on giant dinosaurs such as *Diplodocus*, *Camarasaurus* and *Brachiosaurus*. Most *Allosaurus* fossils have been found in the American Midwest, including the remains of over 65 animals in the Cleveland-Lloyd Dinosaur Quarry, Utah, USA. However, fossils have also been identified in Africa, and a 'dwarf' version has been found in Australia.

SCALE

Eyebrow horns

Long tail

Powerful jaws with long teeth

Long, strong legs and clawed feet

Sharp, clawed hands

FOSSIL FINDS

DINO DATA

Latin name *Ankylosaurus magniventris*

Pronounced an-KIE-low-saw-rus

Name means Stiff Joint Reptile

Group Ankylosaur

Diet Herbivore

Length 7 m

Weight 4 tonnes

Time 70 mya

Where ① North America

SUPER FACT

Ankylosaurus weighed as much as a modern-day elephant. The huge club at the end of its tail weighed 50 kg alone.

MY NOTES AND PICTURES

I'VE SEEN IT...   Books ◯   TV/Films ◯

ANKYLOSAURUS

This dinosaur was covered in thick, bony plates for defence. However, it had a soft, unprotected belly – which meant it walked close to the ground. *Ankylosaurus* had a powerful tail club made up of plates of bone that could be swung with great force, like a hammer. This tail club was nearly one metre across and could deliver a crippling blow to an enemy.

SCALE

Tail club

The tail club was made from pieces of bone that had fused (stuck) together.

Long spikes and bones gave protection from predators

Museums ◯ Internet ◯

FOSSIL FINDS

DINO DATA

Latin name *Apatosaurus ajax*

Pronounced ah-PAT-o-SAW-rus

Name means Deceptive Reptile

Group Sauropod

Diet Herbivore

Length 23 m

Weight 30 tonnes

Time 152 mya

Where ① USA, ② Mexico

SUPER FACT

The head of *Apatosaurus* was tiny, compared to its huge body – hardly bigger than the head of a modern-day pony.

MY NOTES AND PICTURES

The tail had 82 bones – it was used as a whip against enemies

I'VE SEEN IT...   Books ◯   TV/Films ◯

APATOSAURUS

The first fossils of *Apatosaurus* were found in 1877. However in 1879, similar remains were discovered and named *Brontosaurus*. Many years later, it was agreed that both sets of fossils were the same dinosaur, and so the name *Brontosaurus* was dropped. Despite its huge size, *Apatosaurus* could move surprisingly quickly. A sharp, 17-cm-long claw on each front foot may have helped it to balance.

SCALE

Apatosaurus *had no teeth for chewing, it simply pulled leaves from trees with its front teeth.*

Tiny head with peg-like teeth

Massive, pillar-like legs

Museums ⚪ Internet ⚪

FOSSIL FINDS

DINO DATA

Latin name *Avimimus portentosus*

Pronounced AY-vee-MIM-us

Name means Bird Mimic

Group Theropod

Diet Omnivore

Length 1.5 m

Weight 10 kg

Time 95 mya

Where ① Mongolia, ② China

SUPER FACT

Some experts believe there are strong links between *Avimimus* and birds – both have feathers, toothless beaks and slim necks.

MY NOTES AND PICTURES

I'VE SEEN IT...   **Books** ○   **TV/Films** ○

AVIMIMUS

This small dinosaur lived mainly in what is now the Gobi Desert in Mongolia. Its strong, sharp beak pecked for its food of small animals and perhaps plants. Some clues in its fossilized bones suggest that *Avimimus* had feathers, at least on its forearms. However, the arms were too small and weak for flight, so the feathers may have been for warmth or camouflage.

SCALE

Strong, sharp beak for pecking at food

Feathered back

Feathered forearms

Long, strong legs

Museums ◯ Internet ◯

FOSSIL FINDS

DINO DATA

Latin name *Barosaurus lentus*

Pronounced bare-o-SAW-rus

Name means Heavy Reptile

Group Sauropod

Diet Herbivore

Length 25 m

Weight 30 tonnes

Time 155 mya

Where ① USA, ② Africa

SUPER FACT

Despite its huge size, *Barosaurus* may have been able to rear up onto its back legs to feed from the tallest trees.

MY NOTES AND PICTURES

I'VE SEEN IT...   Books ◯   TV/Films ◯

BAROSAURUS

Compared to its long neck and tail, *Barosaurus* had a relatively small body. Its amazingly long neck had 16 to 17 vertebrae, or neck bones, some almost one metre in length. This would have allowed *Barosaurus* to reach the highest branches, needles and leaves of towering tree ferns, gingkoes and conifers. Remains of this long-necked herbivore have been identified at sites in Utah and South Dakota, USA, and possibly in Tanzania, east Africa.

SCALE

Smooth stones called gastroliths were swallowed by Barosaurus to help grind up food in its stomach.

Long neck for reaching the highest leaves

Relatively small body with long tail

Big, bulky legs

Museums ○   Internet ○

FOSSIL FINDS

DINO DATA

Latin name *Baryonyx walkeri*

Pronounced bare-ee-ON-ix

Name means Heavy Claw

Group Theropod

Diet Carnivore

Length 9 m

Weight 2 tonnes

Time 125 mya

Where ① UK

SUPER FACT

Baryonyx may have had more than 100 sharp, saw-like teeth. This is more than most other theropod dinosaurs.

MY NOTES AND PICTURES

I'VE SEEN IT...   **Books** ◯   **TV/Films** ◯

BARYONYX

Long, lean and swift, *Baryonyx* was named for the huge curving claw on each hand. It may have been a fish hunter, wading in rivers and streams to stab its prey with its clawed hands. Its jaws were long and slim, like those of a crocodile. *Baryonyx* was probably a highly intelligent dinosaur.

SCALE

The massive claw was more than 30 cm long.

Long jaws filled with sharp teeth

Clawed hands, each with an extra-large claw

Strong, muscular legs for wading in water

FOSSIL FINDS

DINO DATA

Latin name *Brachiosaurus altithorax*

Pronounced brack-ee-o-SAW-rus

Name means Arm Reptile

Group Sauropod

Diet Herbivore

Length 25 m

Weight 30 to 75 tonnes

Time 150 mya

Where ① North America, ② Europe, ③ Africa

SUPER FACT

Brachiosaurus had similar body proportions to a giraffe, but was more than twice as tall and 50 times heavier.

MY NOTES AND PICTURES

I'VE SEEN IT...   **Books** ◯   **TV/Films** ◯

BRACHIOSAURUS

Brachiosaurus **is still the biggest dinosaur known from fairly complete fossil remains.** It was also one of the most widespread, and its remains have been found in Africa, Europe and North America. Its name of Arm Reptile refers to its long front legs. Along with its flagpole-length neck, these allowed *Brachiosaurus* to reach food 14 m above the ground. There seems to be no reason for the position of its nostrils – rather than at the front of its snout, they were on top of its arched head.

SCALE

Nostrils were positioned on top of the head

Massively long neck

Front legs longer than the back legs

FOSSIL FINDS

SUPER FACT

The bones in the back and neck of *Camarasaurus* were hollow, which is why it was named 'Chambered Reptile'.

DINO DATA

Latin name *Camarasaurus supremus*

Pronounced kam-uh-ruh-SAW-rus

Name means Chambered Reptile

Group Sauropod

Diet Herbivore

Length 20 m

Weight 20 tonnes

Time 152 mya

Where ① USA, ② Mexico

MY NOTES AND PICTURES

I'VE SEEN IT...   Books ○   TV/Films ○

CAMARASAURUS

The neck and tail of *Camarasaurus* were shorter and thicker than many of its cousins such as *Brachiosaurus* and *Diplodocus*. It is one of the best-known of all the big dinosaurs, because so many almost complete fossil skeletons have been found. The skeleton of a young *Camarasaurus* was uncovered in the 1920s, and had nearly every bone in its body lying in the correct position as they were in life – an amazingly rare find.

SCALE

Powerful, bulky body

Small head, and short, thick neck

Sharp claws for defence

FOSSIL FINDS

DINO DATA

Latin name *Caudipteryx zoui*

Pronounced cow-DIP-tuh-riks

Name means Tail Feather

Group Theropod

Diet Omnivore

Length 80 cm

Weight 5 kg

Time 140 mya

Where ① China

SUPER FACT

Fossil remains of *Caudipteryx* indicate that it probably swallowed small stones to help it digest its food.

MY NOTES AND PICTURES

I'VE SEEN IT...   Books ○   TV/Films ○

CAUDIPTERYX

Caudipteryx **was probably a dinosaur with various bird features.** It had a beak, with teeth in the upper jaw, feathers on its body and front limbs, and a long, feathered tail. The front limbs were not used for flying, suggesting that the feathers were for warmth (it may have been warm-blooded), or for colourful displays to attract a mate at breeding time. *Caudipteryx* was about the size of a modern-day turkey.

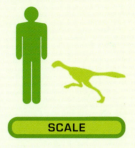

SCALE

Long, feathered tail

Beak-like mouth

Feathered arms

Long, slim legs for swift movement

FOSSIL FINDS

DINO DATA

Latin name *Ceratosaurus nasicornus*

Pronounced sir-RAT-oh-saw-rus

Name means Horned Reptile

Diet Carnivore

Group Theropod

Length 6 m

Weight 850 kg

Time 150 mya

Where ① USA, ② Africa

SUPER FACT

Ceratosaurus had four-fingered hands. This was a very primitive feature, as most Jurassic meat eaters had only three fingers.

MY NOTES AND PICTURES

I'VE SEEN IT...   Books ⭕   TV/Films ⭕

CERATOSAURUS

This dinosaur had a rhino-like horn on its snout and bony lumps above its eyes. A fierce hunter, *Ceratosaurus* lived at the same time and in the same place as its bigger cousin, *Allosaurus*. It could run quickly and its big jaws were filled with sharp, fang-like teeth. The horn on its nose was probably too small to be used as a weapon, but it may have been a sign of a mature adult.

SCALE

Horn on snout

Powerful body

Clawed hands

Strong, muscular legs

FOSSIL FINDS

DINO DATA

Latin name *Coelophysis bauri*

Pronounced see-low-FI-sis

Name means Hollow Form

Group Theropod

Diet Carnivore

Length 3 m

Weight 30 kg

Time 220 mya

Where ① USA

SUPER FACT

In 1998, the space shuttle took a skull of *Coelophysis* into space, where it was taken on board the *Mir* space station.

MY NOTES AND PICTURES

I'VE SEEN IT...   Books ⭕   TV/Films ⭕

COELOPHYSIS

Coelophysis had hollow bones that, along with its very slim build, would have made it extremely light. Its sharp teeth were probably used for grabbing small prey such as lizards and worms. *Coelophysis* was probably the fastest land dinosaur of the Triassic Period and maybe the fastest of all animals of the time, with an estimated top speed of 40 km per hour. Remains of many hundreds of individuals have been found at a site called Ghost Ranch in New Mexico, USA.

SCALE

Small, sharp, teeth

Clawed hands for stabbing prey

Long, fast-running legs

Museums   Internet

FOSSIL FINDS

DINO DATA

Latin name *Compsognathus longipes*

Pronounced komp-sog-NATH-us

Name means Elegant Jaw

Group Theropod

Diet Carnivore

Length 1 m

Weight 2 kg

Time 150 mya

Where ① Germany

SUPER FACT

Compsognathus may have been related to *Archaeopteryx*, the first bird, as its fossils are from the same time and region.

MY NOTES AND PICTURES

I'VE SEEN IT...   Books ◯   TV/Films ◯

COMPSOGNATHUS

The smallest dinosaur, *Compsognathus* is known from fairly complete fossils. Not much larger than a pet cat, it weighed just 2 kg. Its back legs were hardly thicker than a human thumb, the front legs were pencil-slim, and half of its length was made up of a whippy tail. However, this little dinosaur was a fierce predator of small prey such as insects, worms, lizards, and perhaps newly hatched baby dinosaurs.

SCALE

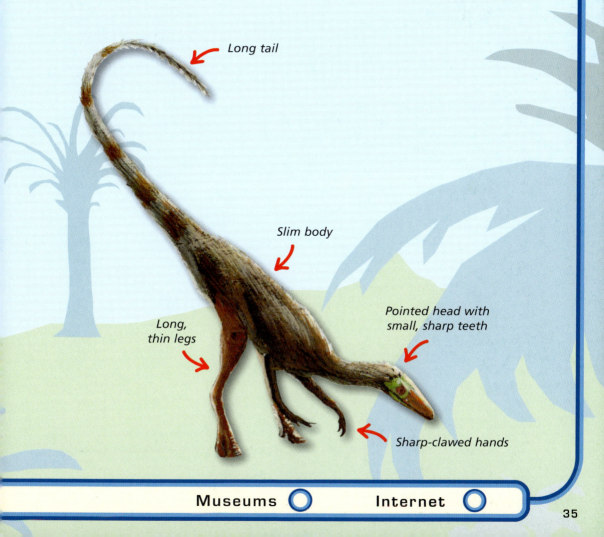

Long tail

Slim body

Long, thin legs

Pointed head with small, sharp teeth

Sharp-clawed hands

Museums ○ Internet ○

FOSSIL FINDS

DINO DATA

Latin name *Corythosaurus casuarius*

Pronounced core-ITH-oh-SAW-rus

Name means Corinthian Helmet Reptile

Group Ornithopod

Diet Herbivore

Length 10 m

Weight 4 tonnes

Time 75 mya

Where ① North America

SUPER FACT

The crest of *Corythosaurus* was probably connected to its nose. This may have allowed it to make noises like an elephant.

MY NOTES AND PICTURES

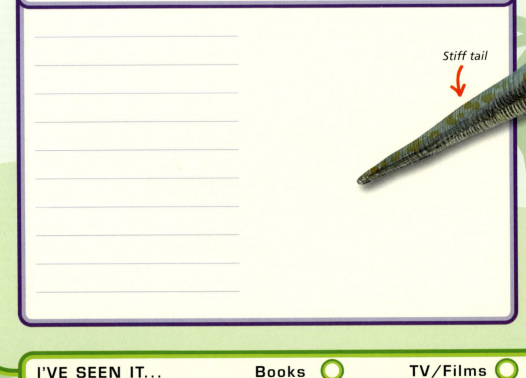

Stiff tail

I'VE SEEN IT...   Books ⚪   TV/Films ⚪

CORYTHOSAURUS

This dinosaur was a hadrosaur – a large 'duckbilled' creature with a bony crest on its head. Its name, Corinthian Helmet Reptile, refers to this crest, which resembled the helmets of soldiers from Corinth, ancient Greece. Hadrosaurs had strong back legs and quite large front legs. They could probably run along on all fours or rear up on their hind legs to feed. Fossil skin of *Corythosaurus* has also been found – it had a strange pebbly texture.

SCALE

Large, bulky body

Bony head crest

Duckbilled-mouth

FOSSIL FINDS

DINO DATA

Latin name *Deinonychus antirrhopus*

Pronounced die-NON-ee-kuss

Name means Terrible Claw

Group Theropod

Diet Carnivore

Length 3 m

Weight 50 kg

Time 120 mya

Where ① USA

SUPER FACT

Deinonychus was one of the most intelligent dinosaurs. It probably hunted in packs, in planned attacks.

MY NOTES AND PICTURES

I'VE SEEN IT...   **Books** ◯   **TV/Films** ◯

DEINONYCHUS

Deinonychus was named after the sharp, curving claw on the second toe of each foot. The joints in the toe allowed the claw to be held off the ground when walking or running, to keep it sharp. It could be swung in a fast slashing motion to attack victims. *Deinonychus* fossils have been found in groups, suggesting that this dinosaur was a pack hunter. Some scientists think that *Deinonychus* could leap onto its prey to attack it.

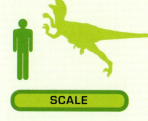

SCALE

Sharp teeth in powerful jaws

Long, flexible tail

Sharp claws for attacking prey

Huge slicing claw on each foot

FOSSIL FINDS

DINO DATA

Latin name *Dilophosaurus wetherilli*

Pronounced die-LOAF-o-SAW-rus

Name means Two-ridged Reptile

Group Theropod

Diet Carnivore

Length 6 m

Weight 500 kg

Time 200 mya

Where ① USA, ② China

SUPER FACT

Dilophosaurus was about the same weight as the biggest polar bears of today – and probably just as fierce.

MY NOTES AND PICTURES

I'VE SEEN IT...   Books ○   TV/Films ○

DILOPHOSAURUS

Dilophosaurus **was one of the biggest early meat-eating dinosaurs.** It was a fast and agile hunter with sharp, curved teeth, easily able to run down prey such as the newly hatched young of large herbivores. It was named Two-ridged Reptile after its head crest, consisting of two narrow, curved plates of bone projecting from the forehead. This crest may have been used to attract a mate, or to help distinguish males from females.

SCALE

Double crest on top of the head

Long, thin legs

Sharp-clawed feet

Museums   Internet

FOSSIL FINDS

SUPER FACT

The body of *Edmontonia* was so well protected, it even had bony armour covering its eyelids.

DINO DATA

Latin name *Edmontonia longiceps*

Pronounced ed-mon-TOE-nee-uh

Name means Of Edmonton

Group Ankylosaur

Diet Herbivore

Length 7 m

Weight 4 tonnes

Time 75 mya

Where ① North America

MY NOTES AND PICTURES

Stiff tail

I'VE SEEN IT...   Books ◯   TV/Films ◯

EDMONTONIA

This heavy dinosaur was covered in bony lumps and plates that acted like a suit of armour. It lacked the large bony lumps at the end of its tail, like a club or hammer, to swing at enemies. Instead, it probably charged and jabbed predators with its neck and shoulder spikes. The beak-like mouth was filled with small teeth. *Edmontonia* probably chewed its food at length and may have kept food in pouches in its mouth. The earliest remains of *Edmontonia* were discovered in 1924 in Canada. The rock layers in which the dinosaur was found are called the Edmonton Formation, and gave this dinosaur its name.

SCALE

Bony plates along the back

Sharp spikes along the shoulders and neck

Short, thick legs

Museums   Internet

FOSSIL FINDS

DINO DATA

Latin name *Eustreptospondylus oxoniensis*

Pronounced u-STREP-toe-spon-DI-lus

Name means Well-curved Spine

Group Theropod

Diet Carnivore

Length 7 m

Weight 250 kg

Time 160 mya

Where ① UK

SUPER FACT

When first discovered, scientists thought that *Eustreptospondylus* was actually the remains of *Megalosaurus*.

MY NOTES AND PICTURES

I'VE SEEN IT...   Books ◯   TV/Films ◯

EUSTREPTOSPONDYLUS

In the Middle Jurassic Period this fierce predator roamed near what is now Oxford, southern England. Much larger than its equivalent carnivores of today, the big cats, *Eustreptospondylus* ran quickly on its strong back legs and four-toed feet, although only three toes touched the ground. Its large head contained long jaws filled with sharp, saw-edged teeth. *Eustreptospondylus* may have hunted stegosaurs and sauropods, as both groups roamed the same region at the time.

Large head, with long jaws filled with sharp teeth

Powerful body

Small arms with three fingers

Strong legs for swift movement

FOSSIL FINDS

SUPER FACT

The head of *Giganotosaurus* measured 1.8 m – as long as an adult person is tall. Its body was as long as a bus.

DINO DATA

Latin name *Giganotosaurus carolinii*

Pronounced jig-an-o-toe-SAW-rus

Name means Giant Southern Reptile

Group Theropod

Diet Carnivore

Length 14 m

Weight 8 tonnes

Time 100 mya

Where ① South America

MY NOTES AND PICTURES

I'VE SEEN IT...   Books ⭕   TV/Films ⭕

GIGANOTOSAURUS

For almost 100 years, *Tyrannosaurus* held the record for being the largest meat eater ever to walk the Earth. In 1994 all this changed when fossils of an even greater carnivore were discovered in the Patagonia region of Argentina. Named *Giganotosaurus*, this theropod was huge, and its teeth were more than 20 cm in length. *Giganotosaurus* preyed on the massive sauropod dinosaurs.

SCALE

Huge head, powerful
jaws and long teeth

Sharp-clawed
hands

Large, powerful
legs and feet

FOSSIL FINDS

SUPER FACT

Able to move at speed, *Herrerasaurus* may be the oldest meat-eating dinosaur ever discovered.

DINO DATA

Latin name *Herrerasaurus ischigualastensis*

Pronounced huh-RARE-uh-SAW-rus

Name means Herrera's Reptile

Group Theropod

Diet Carnivore

Length 4 m

Weight 100 kg

Time 225 mya

Where ① Argentina

MY NOTES AND PICTURES

Long tail for balance

HERRERASAURUS

Herrerasaurus **was named after Argentinean goat-herder, Victorino Herrera, who discovered its fossils.** It is one of several very early dinosaurs from the Middle to Late Triassic Period found in what is now South America. A powerful predator, *Herrerasaurus* had long, narrow jaws filled with sharp, back-curving teeth, and strong rear legs allowing it to move quickly. It probably hunted small animals such as lizards, insects and other reptiles.

SCALE

Sharp teeth in long jaws

Clawless hands

Long, strong legs for speed

Museums   Internet

FOSSIL FINDS

DINO DATA

Latin name *Hypsilophodon foxii*

Pronounced hip-sih-LOFF-oh-don

Name means High-ridge Tooth

Group Ornithopod

Diet Herbivore

Length 2.5 m

Weight 25 kg

Time 125 mya

Where ① North America, ② Europe

SUPER FACT

Early dinosaur experts thought that *Hypsilophodon* might have lived in trees – a theory that has now been proved as untrue.

MY NOTES AND PICTURES

HYPSILOPHODON

This small, fast plant eater may have lived in herds like modern-day antelopes. It had a long, straight tail to help it balance and strong, sturdy claws that it probably used to scrabble and dig in soil for seeds and roots. Several fossils of *Hypsilophodon* have been found together, which may mean that a whole group or herd probably died in a flood, or trying to cross a river.

SCALE

Small skull and beaked mouth

Long rear legs

The clawed hands were perfectly adapted for digging out food from the soil.

EARLY CRETACEOUS PERIOD 144–98 MYA

FOSSIL FINDS

DINO DATA

Latin name *Iguanodon anglicusi*

Pronounced ig-WHA-no-don

Name means Iguana Tooth

Group Ornithopod

Diet Herbivore

Length 10 m

Weight 4 to 5 tonnes

Time 110 mya

Where ① North America, ② Europe, ③ Africa

SUPER FACT

In early reconstructions, the spike of *Iguanodon* was placed on its nose, as scientists didn't realize it was part of its hand.

MY NOTES AND PICTURES

I'VE SEEN IT...   Books ◯   TV/Films ◯

IGUANODON

Iguanodon is one of the best-studied dinosaurs as so many of its fossils have been found. At one coal mine in Belgium, the remains of about 40 almost complete skeletons jumbled together were found. This suggests that a herd died, perhaps while trying to cross a river. On each 'thumb' (first front toe) *Iguanodon* had a sharp spike for jabbing at enemies. This dinosaur weighed about the same as an African elephant.

SCALE

Large, bulky body

Beaked mouth for eating plants

Strong rear legs

The thumb spike was used in defence and the fingers grasped food.

FOSSIL FINDS

DINO DATA

Latin name *Janenschia robusta*

Pronounced jay-NEN-she-uh

Name means For Janensch

Group Sauropod

Diet Herbivore

Length 20 m

Weight 25 tonnes

Time 156 mya

Where ① Africa

SUPER FACT

There is a possibility that *Janenschia* may have been covered in bony plates for protection.

MY NOTES AND PICTURES

I'VE SEEN IT...   Books ◯   TV/Films ◯

JANENSCHIA

This huge herbivore was named after **Werner Janensch, a German palaeontologist who discovered its remains.** It walked on four thick, pillar-like legs and its rear feet may have had claws. Like other large herbivore dinosaurs, *Janenschia* probably had a very powerful heart to pump blood around its enormous body. Only a few leg fossils of *Janenschia* have been found – one thigh bone alone was 1.4 m long.

SCALE

Tiny head

Extremely long neck for grazing from the tallest trees

Huge, thick legs

FOSSIL FINDS

DINO DATA

Latin name *Jobaria tiguidensis*

Pronounced jo-BAH-ria

Name means For Jobar

Group Sauropod

Diet Herbivore

Length 21 m

Weight 20 tonnes

Time 135 mya

Where ① Africa

SUPER FACT

When *Jobaria* was alive, 135 mya, the Sahara Desert would have been covered with trees and lakes.

MY NOTES AND PICTURES

I'VE SEEN IT...   Books ◯   TV/Films ◯

JOBARIA

A huge sauropod from the Early Cretaceous Period, *Jobaria* had a relatively short neck and spoon-like teeth. It may have been able to rear up onto its hind legs for feeding or in defence. A near complete skeleton of this herbivore was found in 1997 in Niger, Africa. *Jobaria* was named after Jobar, a mythical creature of the Tuareg people from North Africa.

SCALE

Flexible neck

Long tail

May have reared up on hind legs to feed

FOSSIL FINDS

DINO DATA

Latin name *Kentrosaurus longispinus*

Pronounced ken-TROH-saw-rus

Name means Spiky Lizard

Group Stegosaur

Diet Herbivore

Length 5 m

Weight 2 tonnes

Time 155 mya

Where ① Africa

SUPER FACT

Some of the best fossils of *Kentrosaurus* were destroyed in the bombing raids on Germany during World War II.

MY NOTES AND PICTURES

Stiff tail

I'VE SEEN IT...   **Books** ◯   **TV/Films** ◯

KENTROSAURUS

Like other members of the stegosaur group, *Kentrosaurus* had a double row of long, bony plates and spikes for protection. It had a beak-shaped mouth for nipping plants and an arched back. The tiny head held a tiny brain – this dinosaur wasn't very intelligent. It moved slowly, eating low-lying plants most of the time.

SCALE

Two rows of long spikes along the back

Double row of bony plates along the neck

Clawed, hoof-like feet

FOSSIL FINDS

DINO DATA

Latin name *Lambeosaurus lambei*

Pronounced lam-bee-o-SAW-rus

Name means Lambe's Reptile

Group Ornithopod

Diet Herbivore

Length 15 m

Weight 5 tonnes

Time 77 mya

Where ① Canada, ② Mexico

SUPER FACT

Lambeosaurus weighed more than an elephant, but could run slowly for several hours. It is the largest duckbilled dinosaur.

MY NOTES AND PICTURES

I'VE SEEN IT...   **Books** ◯   **TV/Films** ◯

LAMBEOSAURUS

*L*ambeosaurus had a wide, flat, toothless mouth that was similar to a duck's beak. It gathered plants that were then crushed to a pulp by rows of sharp-ridged cheek teeth. A hollow head crest projected at a right angle from its head, which may have identified males from females, or may even have been used to call to each other during the mating season. This dinosaur was named after Lawrence Lambe, an early Canadian fossil hunter.

SCALE

Stiff tail for balance

Big, bulky body with bumpy skin

Hollow crest on top of head

Strong back legs

Beaky mouth filled with hundreds of teeth

FOSSIL FINDS

SUPER FACT

Australia used to be much colder than it is today, so *Leaellynasaura* may have hibernated in the cold season.

DINO DATA

Latin name *Leaellynasaura amicagraphica*

Pronounced lee-ell-in-uh-SAW-ruh

Name means Leaellyn's Reptile

Group Ornithopod

Diet Herbivore

Length 2 m

Weight 10 kg

Time 120 mya

Where ① Australia

MY NOTES AND PICTURES

I'VE SEEN IT...   Books ◯   TV/Films ◯

LEAELLYNASAURA

This small plant eater was named Lea Ellyn's Reptile after the young daughter of its discoverer. Its fossils come from the famous Dinosaur Cove coastal cliff site near Melbourne, Australia. *Leaellynasaura* had large eye sockets, and along with plant fossils from the site, this suggests that it may have lived in thick forest and so had big eyes to see in the gloom. It had a beak-like mouth for eating vegetation such as ferns, cycads and flowering plants, which were spreading around the world at the time.

SCALE

Strong jaws and beak-like mouth

Long legs for running fast

Clawed hands

FOSSIL FINDS

DINO DATA

Latin name *Maiasaura peeblesorum*

Pronounced my-uh-SAW-ruh

Name means Good Mother Reptile

Group Ornithopod

Diet Herbivore

Length 9 m

Weight 3 to 4 tonnes

Time 80 mya

Where ① North America

SUPER FACT

Maiasaura was the first dinosaur in space. A piece of bone and an eggshell were sent into space in 1985.

MY NOTES AND PICTURES

I'VE SEEN IT...   Books ⬤   TV/Films ⬤

MAIASAURA

This large plant eater was a duckbilled dinosaur. In the 1970s, huge collections of *Maiasaura* skeletons of all ages were found in Montana, USA. This showed that these dinosaurs bred in groups called colonies, and each laid its eggs in a nest scooped out of earth. The teeth of the babies were worn from eating, yet their limb bones were not yet developed enough for walking. The parent dinosaur may have brought food to them in the nest, which is why the name *Maiasaura* means Good Mother Reptile.

SCALE

Large, bulky body

Long hind legs

Beaked mouth with lots of cheek teeth

FOSSIL FINDS

DINO DATA

Latin name *Megalosaurus bucklandii*

Pronounced MEG-ah-low-saw-rus

Name means Big Reptile

Group Theropod

Diet Carnivore

Length 9 m

Weight 1 tonne

Time 160 mya

Where ① UK

SUPER FACT

Early scientists thought that *Megalosaurus* walked on four legs like other reptiles – today we know it walked on two.

MY NOTES AND PICTURES

I'VE SEEN IT...   Books ◯   TV/Films ◯

MEGALOSAURUS

This dinosaur was a big meat eater. It had small front arms and a huge skull. Its long, stiff tail was kept off the ground, and *Megalosaurus* was able to run at speed over short distances. The sharp teeth were curved, with a saw-toothed edge. It had inward-pointing toes, and strong sharp claws on both feet and hands. When *Megalosaurus* was discovered in 1822, the word 'dinosaur' did not even exist. It was not until 1841 that dinosaurs were recognized as a new group of extinct reptiles.

SCALE

Powerful body

Long, sharp teeth in powerful jaws

Sharp-clawed hands

Long, strong back legs for swift movement

FOSSIL FINDS

DINO DATA

Latin name *Muttaburrasaurus langdoni*

Pronounced mut-a-burr-a-SAW-rus

Name means Muttaburra Reptile

Group Ornithopod

Diet Herbivore

Length 7 m

Weight 3 tonnes

Time 110 mya

Where ① Australia

SUPER FACT

Large spikes on the hands of *Muttaburrasaurus* may have been used to stab predators or to pick up food.

MY NOTES AND PICTURES

Long tail

I'VE SEEN IT...   **Books** ◯   **TV/Films** ◯

MUTTABURRASAURUS

Muttaburrasaurus was a cousin of Iguanodon. It had a bulge on its toothless, horned snout that reached from its nostrils to its eyes. This may have been used to make loud calling sounds. It probably moved on two legs, but may have been able to run on all four. To feed, it would have been able to stand on all four legs in order to reach low bushes or rear up on its back legs to reach higher trees. Like *Iguanodon*, *Muttaburrasaurus* had large thumb spikes.

SCALE

Bump on the snout

Long, powerful legs

Clawed hands with a thumb spike

FOSSIL FINDS

DINO DATA

Latin name *Ornitholestes hermanni*

Pronounced or-ni-thoe-LESS-tees

Name means Bird Robber

Group Theropod

Diet Carnivore

Length 2 m

Weight 15 kg

Time 144 mya

Where ① USA

SUPER FACT

Ornitholestes had exceptionally long fingers – ideal for grabbing baby dinosaurs newly hatched from their eggs.

MY NOTES AND PICTURES

I'VE SEEN IT...   Books ◯   TV/Films ◯

ORNITHOLESTES

This lightweight, meat-eating dinosaur was named Bird Robber because it was originally believed to have chased and eaten early types of birds, such as *Archaeopteryx*. This fact is now in debate as the fossils of these two creatures, both from the Late Jurassic Period, were found thousands of kilometres apart. The long, powerful arms and hands had curved claws like bent daggers – ideal for catching small prey. The rear legs were also long and slim, but very powerful, allowing *Ornitholestes* to run fast. Only one fossilized skeleton has been discovered, so there is still more to learn about this small dinosaur.

SCALE

Crest on the head

Light body

Long tail

Long back legs

Clawed hands, with one very long finger

FOSSIL FINDS

DINO DATA

Latin name *Ornithomimus velox*

Pronounced or-NITH-o-MEE-mus

Name means Bird Mimic

Group Theropod

Diet Omnivore

Length 4 m

Weight 150 kg

Time 77 mya

Where ① North America

SUPER FACT

Ornithomimus could probably reach speeds of 70 km per hour – the same speed as a modern-day ostrich.

MY NOTES AND PICTURES

Long, stiff tail

ORNITHOMIMUS

Ornithomimus **is thought to be omnivorous, eating both plants and small animals.** Its mouth was shaped like a bird's beak and made out of a tough, strong, horny substance like our fingernails. It pecked at all kinds of foods such as seeds, worms and bugs, but its head is thought to be too small to be able to hunt bigger prey. The long arms with their clawed fingers could grasp food to eat. It was able to run fast to escape predators.

SCALE

Beaked mouth

Long neck

Long arms with clawed hands

Long, strong fast-running legs

Museums ◯   Internet ◯

FOSSIL FINDS

SUPER FACT

Oviraptor had two bony spikes inside its mouth that it may have used to crack eggs when it closed its jaws.

DINO DATA

Latin name *Oviraptor philoceratops*

Pronounced o-vee-RAP-tor

Name means Egg Thief

Group Theropod

Diet Omnivore

Length 2 m

Weight 30 kg

Time 83 mya

Where ① Asia

MY NOTES AND PICTURES

I'VE SEEN IT...   Books ◯   TV/Films ◯

OVIRAPTOR

*O*viraptor **gained the name Egg Thief as the first of its fossils were found lying among the broken eggs of another dinosaur.** Instead of teeth, *Oviraptor* had a strong, curved beak, like that of a parrot or eagle, which was used to crack open eggs. On its forehead was a tall, rounded piece of bone, like a crest, that may have been to signify dominance in a group. *Oviraptor* fossils have been found in the Gobi Desert in Asia.

SCALE

Head crest

Parrot-like mouth

Long, powerful legs for running

Long arms and claws for grabbing prey

FOSSIL FINDS

SUPER FACT

Pachycephalosaurus had five fingers on each hand – a primitive feature for a dinosaur that appeared so late.

DINO DATA

Latin name *Pachycephalosaurus wyomingensis*

Pronounced pack-ee-KEF-ah-low-saw-rus

Name means Thick-head Lizard

Group Pachycephalosaur

Diet Herbivore

Length 8 m

Weight 1 tonne

Time 76 mya

Where ① USA

MY NOTES AND PICTURES

I'VE SEEN IT...   Books ◯   TV/Films ◯

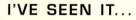

PACHYCEPHALOSAURUS

This strange-looking dinosaur belonged to the 'bonehead' group. It had a large bony dome on top of its skull, which protected its skull in possible headbutting contests. However, scientists now think that this is unlikely as the adult skulls probably didn't stand up to such heavy use. Instead, these dinosaurs may have butted each other, or enemies, on the shoulder or flank.

Thick, bony skull

Long tail for balance

Powerful legs for swift movement

Five-fingered hands

Museums   Internet

FOSSIL FINDS

DINO DATA

Latin name *Parasaurolophus walkeri*

Pronounced pa-ra-saw-ROL-off-us

Name means Beside Ridged Reptile

Group Ornithopod

Diet Herbivore

Length 12 m

Weight 3 tonnes

Time 75 mya

Where ① North America

SUPER FACT

When scientists first discovered *Parasaurolophus*, they thought its head crest was a giant snorkel.

MY NOTES AND PICTURES

I'VE SEEN IT...   Books ◯   TV/Films ◯

PARASAUROLOPHUS

Of the many kinds of duckbilled dinosaurs, the longest head crest belonged to *Parasaurolophus*. This strange structure stuck up and back from the skull for almost 2 m. It was not solid bone, but contained two air tubes that led from the nostrils, passed up inside the front of the crest, looped over at the top and then passed down again, on the way to the lungs. This dinosaur may have been able to blow air through its crest to make a low honking sound, like a trombone or even a foghorn.

SCALE

Hollow head crest

Beaked mouth

Bulky body with bumpy skin

FOSSIL FINDS

DINO DATA

Latin name *Plateosaurus engelhardti*

Pronounced plate-e-o-SAW-rus

Name means Flat Reptile

Group Prosauropod

Diet Herbivore

Length 8 m

Weight 1 tonne

Time 210 mya

Where ① Europe

SUPER FACT

The thumbs of *Plateosaurus* ended in a large spike that was used for jabbing at enemies and grasping food.

MY NOTES AND PICTURES

Long, strong tail

I'VE SEEN IT...   Books ◯   TV/Films ◯

PLATEOSAURUS

Plateosaurus **was one of the first large dinosaurs.** It is well known from many skeletons that have been unearthed at various sites in Europe, including France, Switzerland and Germany. Its long body, sturdy hips and powerful, weighty tail could mean that it reared up on its hind limbs and leaned back, using its muscular tail for support. In this way it could reach tree ferns and other plant food 5 m above the ground.

SCALE

The flexible front feet could be greatly extended to pull down branches to eat.

Long, bendy neck

Large, bulky body

Museums ◯ Internet ◯

FOSSIL FINDS

SUPER FACT

A primitive ankylosaur, the first fossils of *Polacanthus* were found on a cliff face on the Isle of Wight in England.

DINO DATA

Latin name *Polacanthus foxii*

Pronounced pol-a-KAN-thus

Name means Many Spikes

Group Ankylosaur

Diet Herbivore

Length 5 m

Weight 1 tonne

Time 125 mya

Where ① UK, ② Europe

MY NOTES AND PICTURES

I'VE SEEN IT...   Books ◯   TV/Films ◯

POLACANTHUS

One of the early armoured dinosaurs, *Polacanthus* was a huge, lumbering herbivore. The formation of its protective spikes is not clear, but they may have jutted out from the shoulders. Although covered in bony plates and spikes, its soft underbelly made it vulnerable to attack. It is not certain whether *Polacanthus* had a tail club for swinging at enemies. Its fossils have been found in southern England and at various sites on mainland Europe.

SCALE

Long, spiky tail

Spikes of bone for protection

Small head

Museums ⬤ Internet ⬤

FOSSIL FINDS

DINO DATA

Latin name *Procompsognathus triassicus*

Pronounced pro-comp-sog-NATH-us

Name means Before Compsognathus

Group Theropod

Diet Carnivore

Length 1 m

Weight 2.5 kg

Time 215 mya

Where ① Germany

SUPER FACT

Procompsognathus was about the same weight as a domestic cat – but it was much slimmer and twice as long.

MY NOTES AND PICTURES

I'VE SEEN IT...   Books ◯   TV/Films ◯

PROCOMPSOGNATHUS

Procompsognathus **was a lightweight, agile meat eater.** Its teeth were more suited to hunting live prey, such as newly hatched dinosaurs, rather than for scavenging. Its tail formed almost half of its total length, and instead of being whip-like, it was probably quite stiff. The name '*Pro* (before) *Compsognathus*' is true in that the smaller *Compsognathus* lived later, and the two dinosaurs were similar in shape. However, it does not not mean that *Compsognathus* was descended from *Procompsognathus*, since more than 60 million years separated them.

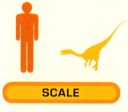

SCALE

Long, stiff tail

Lightweight body

Small, slim head filled with sharp teeth

Sharp-clawed hands

Museums ○   Internet ○

FOSSIL FINDS

DINO DATA

Latin name *Protoceratops andrewsi*

Pronounced pro-toe-SAIR-o-tops

Name means First Horned Face

Group Ceratopsian

Diet Herbivore

Length 2 m

Weight 220 kg

Time 82 mya

Where ① Asia

SUPER FACT

A fossilized *Protoceratops* has been found locked in battle with a *Velociraptor*, fighting to the death.

MY NOTES AND PICTURES

I'VE SEEN IT... Books ○ TV/Films ○

PROTOCERATOPS

Protoceratops **lived in the region that is now the Gobi Desert in Asia.** This ancestor of the ceratopsian (horn-faced) dinosaurs resembles the more famous member, *Triceratops*, but it was actually much smaller. Its neck frill was also small and plain compared to those of the later ceratopsians. *Protoceratops* had a tough beak used for cropping vegetation and two small horn-like bumps on the sides of its face.

SCALE

This fossil shows the frill-like neck bones and beaky mouth of Protoceratops.

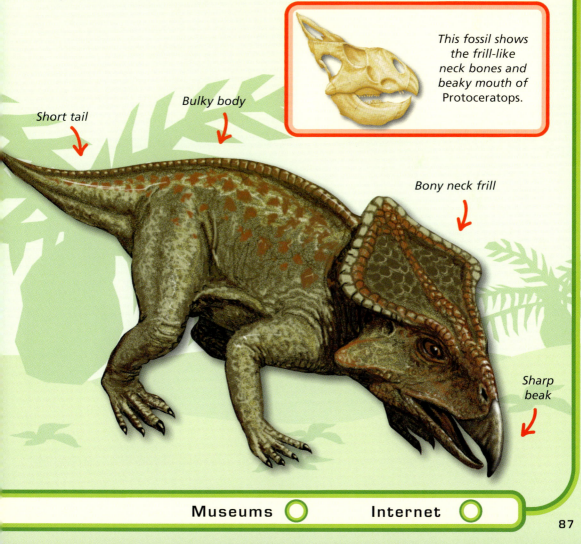

Short tail

Bulky body

Bony neck frill

Sharp beak

FOSSIL FINDS

DINO DATA

Latin name *Psittacosaurus mongolensis*

Pronounced sit-ACK-oh-SAW-rus

Name means Parrot Reptile

Group Ceratopsian

Diet Herbivore

Length 2 m

Weight 40 kg

Time 120 mya

Where ① Asia

SUPER FACT

Fossil evidence shows that when first hatched, the young *Psittacosaurus* were hardly bigger than a human hand.

MY NOTES AND PICTURES

I'VE SEEN IT...   Books ◯   TV/Films ◯

PSITTACOSAURUS

Psittacosaurus was an early type of horned dinosaur (ceratopsian), although it had not yet developed the nose horn or neck frill. In 2004 an amazing discovery in China showed the remains of an adult *Psittacosaurus*, a small parrot-beaked plant eater, surrounded by more than 30 young. This suggests the adult was caring for the young when they all died in a sudden disaster.

SCALE

Long spiny tail

Light, slim body

Long, strong hindlegs

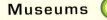

Museums   Internet

FOSSIL FINDS

DINO DATA

Latin name *Riojasaurus incertis*

Pronounced ree-O-ha-SAW-rus

Name means Rioja Reptile

Group Prosauropod

Diet Herbivore

Length 10 m

Weight 1 tonne

Time 215 mya

Where ① South America

SUPER FACT

Riojasaurus did not chew its food. It swallowed stones to help grind the food up in its huge stomach.

MY NOTES AND PICTURES

Long tail

I'VE SEEN IT...   Books ○   TV/Films ○

RIOJASAURUS

The remains of *Riojasaurus*, one of the first truly large dinosaurs, date back to 220 mya. They were first discovered in the 1920s in the La Rioja district of Argentina, hence the name. Further fossils have since been found of more than 20 individuals. *Riojasaurus* probably moved on all fours but perhaps reared up on its back legs, like *Plateosaurus*, to reach leaves several metres off the ground.

SCALE

Small head

Large, bulky body

Long, bendy neck

FOSSIL FINDS

DINO DATA

Latin name *Saltasaurus loricatus*

Pronounced salt-ah-SAW-rus

Name means Salta Reptile

Group Sauropod

Diet Herbivore

Length 12 m

Weight 10 tonnes

Time 70 mya

Where ① Argentina

SUPER FACT

Some of the bony plates on the body of *Saltasaurus* may have had sharp spikes sticking out from them.

MY NOTES AND PICTURES

Whip-like tail

I'VE SEEN IT...   **Books** ○   **TV/Films** ○

SALTASAURUS

One of the last great sauropods, *Saltasaurus* is unusual in this group as it had protective bony lumps and plates on its skin. These ranged from the size of a human hand down to the size of a shirt button. It also had a short neck, for a sauropod, a muscular tail and a low stocky body. *Saltasaurus* may have been able to rear up onto its back legs to eat leaves from the tallest trees.

SCALE

Tiny mouth

Bulky body covered in protective bony plates

Short neck

Pillar-like legs

Museums ◯ Internet ◯

FOSSIL FINDS

DINO DATA

Latin name *Shunosaurus lii*

Pronounced shoo-no-SAW-rus

Name means Shuo Reptile

Group Sauropod

Diet Herbivore

Length 11 m

Weight 10 tonnes

Time 170 mya

Where ① China

SUPER FACT

Shunosaurus may have lived to be more than 100 years of age. It is the only sauropod dinosaur to have a spiked tail.

MY NOTES AND PICTURES

I'VE SEEN IT...   Books ○   TV/Films ○

SHUNOSAURUS

A smaller sauropod, *Shunosaurus* had a shorter neck, but still had the bulky body and long tail of its group. Its most noticeable feature was a tail club made of enlarged bones, possibly armed with several spikes. This would be an effective defensive weapon when swung at attacking carnivores. Remains of *Shunosaurus* include five skulls, which is unusual as the skull is among the smallest, most fragile part of a sauropod's body and rarely fossilizes.

SCALE

Spiked tail used for defence

Big, bulky body

Short legs

Museums ○   Internet ○

FOSSIL FINDS

DINO DATA

Latin name *Spinosaurus aegyptiacus*

Pronounced spin-o-SAW-rus

Name means Spiny Reptile

Diet Carnivore

Group Theropod

Length 15 m

Weight 3 tonnes

Time 98 mya

Where ① North Africa

SUPER FACT

The teeth of *Spinosaurus* were as sharp as knives, but they were straight – not curved like other dinosaur teeth.

MY NOTES AND PICTURES

I'VE SEEN IT...   Books ◯   TV/Films ◯

SPINOSAURUS

A large meat eater, *Spinosaurus* had a long, crocodile-like head similar to that of *Baryonyx*. Its teeth were slim and sharp suggesting that it scavenged for food on rotting carcasses. It has given its name to a group of therapod dinosaurs, the spinosaurs. *Spinosaurus* also had a distinctive 'sail' on its back, formed of skin held up by long, bony rods. The sail was almost 2 m tall and may have been a way of controlling body temperature, or to attract a mate at breeding time.

SCALE

Large sail on the back held up by long, bony rods

Long, slim jaws filled with sharp teeth

Long, powerful legs

Clawed hands

FOSSIL FINDS

DINO DATA

Latin name *Stegosaurus armatus*

Pronounced steg-o-SAW-rus

Name means Roof Reptile

Group Stegosaur

Diet Herbivore

Length 9 m

Weight 3 tonnes

Time 155 mya

Where ① USA

SUPER FACT

Stegosaurus is thought to have had the smallest brain for its body size of all the dinosaurs – about the size of a golf ball.

MY NOTES AND PICTURES

Spiky tail for defence

I'VE SEEN IT...   Books ◯   TV/Films ◯

STEGOSAURUS

One of the puzzles about dinosaurs is the reason for the tall, diamond-shaped back plates of *Stegosaurus*. They were made of lightweight bone probably covered by skin, and were of little use for protection. Perhaps they worked as heat absorbers to soak up the sun's warmth so that this herbivore could get moving more quickly in the morning than other cold-blooded dinosaurs. *Stegosaurus* had a spiked tail that it used to swing at enemies.

SCALE

Large plates running in two rows down the back and tail

Tiny head

FOSSIL FINDS

DINO DATA

Latin name *Syntarsus rhodesiensis*

Pronounced sin-TAR-sus

Name means Fused Ankle

Group Theropod

Diet Carnivore

Length 2 m

Weight 15 kg

Time 200 mya

Where ① USA, ② Africa

SUPER FACT

The head crest of *Syntarsus* has been found on fossils from North America, but it is missing from those found in Africa.

MY NOTES AND PICTURES

I'VE SEEN IT...   **Books** ◯   **TV/Films** ◯

SYNTARSUS

This fast-moving dinosaur was one of the first meat eaters of the Triassic Period. It was a swift runner and was able to grab and hold down its prey with its long, sharp-clawed hands. Its jaws were filled with lots of sharp teeth. The bones of several *Syntarsus* have been found in Zimbabwe, Africa, and this suggests that the dinosaur may have lived in herds. The four-toed feet were fused (joined) at the ankle, giving the dinosaur its name. *Syntarsus* is a good example of how dinosaurs spread from North America to Africa.

Crest on head

Long jaws filled with sharp teeth

Long tail

Slim, light body

Large, clawed hands

Museums ◯ Internet ◯

FOSSIL FINDS

DINO DATA

Latin name *Triceratops horridus*

Pronounced try-SAIR-o-tops

Name means Three–horned Face

Group Ceratopsian

Diet Herbivore

Length 9 m

Weight 5 tonnes

Time 65 mya

Where ① USA

SUPER FACT

Triceratops was twice the size of a modern rhinoceros. It also lived in herds, which protected it from enemies.

MY NOTES AND PICTURES

I'VE SEEN IT...   **Books** ○   **TV/Films** ○

TRICERATOPS

The biggest of the horned dinosaurs, or ceratopsians, *Triceratops* was no easy victim for predators such as *Tyrannosaurus*. Its eyebrow horns were almost one metre long and its wide, bony neck frill was larger than a dining table. *Triceratops* would have charged with twice the bulk and power of today's rhinoceros. But most of the time it probably snipped off vegetation with its sharp parrot-like beak, and munched this food with its many sharp-ridged cheek teeth.

Large bony neck frill

Long brow horns

Sharp, toothless beak

FOSSIL FINDS

DINO DATA

Latin name *Troodon formosus*

Pronounced true-don

Name means Wounding Tooth

Group Theropod

Diet Carnivore

Length 3 m

Weight 50 kg

Time 76 mya

Where ① USA

SUPER FACT

Troodon had the largest brain, compared to body size, of any dinosaur. It was named from the evidence of a fossil tooth.

MY NOTES AND PICTURES

I'VE SEEN IT...   **Books** ◯   **TV/Films** ◯

TROODON

This big-brained dinosaur was a slender, lightweight hunter of small lizards, birds, mammals and other small prey. Its fossils show that its eyes were large, and from the shape of the brain cavity inside the skull, it had keen senses of sight, hearing and smell. *Troodon* would have stood chest-high to a person and could probably move at speed. Its name Wounding Tooth refers to its saw-edged teeth.

SCALE

Long, whippy tail

Narrow jaws

The skull shows large cavities for the eyes suggesting that Troodon *was a night hunter.*

Feathered arms

Long, curved claw on foot

Slim legs

FOSSIL FINDS

DINO DATA

Latin name *Tuojiangosaurus multispinus*

Pronounced Two-oh-jee-ang-oh-SAW-rus

Name means: Tou River Reptile

Group Stegosaur

Diet Herbivore

Length 7 m

Weight 1 tonne

Time 150 mya

Where ① China

SUPER FACT

The plates on the back of *Tuojiangosaurus* were probably used to stop its body temperature getting too hot.

MY NOTES AND PICTURES

I'VE SEEN IT...   **Books** ◯   **TV/Films** ◯

TUOJIANGOSAURUS

Named after the Tuo River in China, this plant eater showed how the stegosaurs had spread to most continents by the Late Jurassic Period. Like other stegosaurs, *Tuojiangosaurus* had tall triangular plates of bone along its back. These probably stuck upright in two rows. The birdlike beak cropped low vegetation, and the four large spikes at the end of the tail were arranged as two V-shapes in a formidable defensive weapon.

SCALE

Four-spiked tail

Double row of bony plates

Small head with beak-shaped mouth

FOSSIL FINDS

DINO DATA

Latin name *Tyrannosaurus rex*

Pronounced tie-Ran-o-SAW-rus

Name means Tyrant Reptile

Group Theropod

Diet Carnivore

Length 12 m

Weight 6 tonnes

Time 67 mya

Where ① USA

SUPER FACT

The teeth of *Tyrannosaurus* were 15 to 25 cm in length and were powerful enough to crunch through bone.

MY NOTES AND PICTURES

I'VE SEEN IT...   **Books** ◯   **TV/Films** ◯

TYRANNOSAURUS REX

Famous for being the biggest hunting animal ever to walk the land, *Tyrannosaurus* has lost this record to *Giganotosaurus*. However, *Tyrannosaurus* remains the dinosaur we love to fear. Its mouth opened so wide that it could have easily swallowed a ten-year-old child. This great predator lived in North America and was one of the last dinosaurs to appear.

SCALE

Massive head measuring 1.6 m in length

Small, useless arms

Huge feet and powerful legs

Museums ◯ Internet ◯

FOSSIL FINDS

DINO DATA

Latin name *Velociraptor mongoliensis*

Pronounced ve-LOSS-ih-RAP-tor

Name means Swift Robber

Group Theropod

Diet Carnivore

Length 2 m

Weight 20 kg

Time 85 mya

Where ① Central Asia

SUPER FACT

Although it was a fierce meat eater, *Velociraptor* was no bigger than a modern-day Great Dane dog.

MY NOTES AND PICTURES

I'VE SEEN IT...   Books ◯   TV/Films ◯

VELOCIRAPTOR

This dinosaur was a powerful, agile meat eater. With a super-sharp claw on each foot, it was capable of cutting metre-long gashes into its prey. It lived in what is now the dry scrub and desert of Mongolia, Central Asia. *Velociraptor* probably ran fast and could leap great distances on its powerful back legs.

SCALE

Sharp, curved teeth

Long tail for balance

Long legs for leaping onto victims

Huge sharp claw for tearing at prey

Museums

Internet

GLOSSARY

Camouflaged When an animal is shaped, coloured or patterned to blend in with its surroundings.

Carnivore An animal that eats only or mostly meat.

Ceratopsian The family of dinosaurs that was characterized by having horns on their heads.

Coprolites Fossilized dinosaur droppings.

Dinosaur A group of reptiles characterized by having legs that were tucked directly underneath their bodies.

Evolve The gradual change in which animals and plants adapt to survive the changing world around them.

Fossil A part of an animal or plant that has been preserved, usually in rock.

Gastrolith A stone swallowed by some dinosaurs to help with the digestion of tough plant foods.

Herbivore An animal that eats only or mostly plants.

Nodosaur The family of dinosaurs that had bony armour and spikes, but no tail clubs.

Ornithischian One of two main types of dinosaur. Ornithischians had hips shaped like those of modern-day birds. All ornithischian dinosaurs were plant eaters.

Pachycephalosaur The family of dinosaurs that had very thick skull bones.

Palaeontologist A scientist who studies prehistoric animals and plants.

Predator A meat-eating animal that hunts and kills other creatures for food.

Prosauropod The family of dinosaurs that could walk on two or four legs and ate plants, which lived before the sauropods.

Raptor A group of small, fast-moving theropods that had a claw on the hind foot that was much larger than the other claws.

Reptile A group of animals characterized by having scaly skin and laying eggs.

Saurischian One of two main types of dinosaur. Saurischians had hips shaped like those of modern lizards.

Sauropod The family of plant-eating dinosaurs that walked on four legs and reached enormous sizes.

Scavenge To feed on meat from the body of an animal that has died from disease or other natural causes.

Stegosaur The family of plant-eating dinosaurs that had plates or spikes growing along their backs.

Theropod A general term for two-legged meat-eating dinosaurs.

Vertebrae The bones that are joined together to form the backbone.

Warm-blooded An animal that is able to generate its own body heat, rather than absorbing heat from its surroundings.